The B & B
COOKBOOK

The B & B COOKBOOK

Extraordinary Recipes from an Exceptional B & B

Plus tips and advice for new
and experienced B & B owners

by

Bonnie Williams-Paquette

Eloquent Books
An imprint of Strategic Book Group
P.O. Box 333 Durham CT 06422
www.StrategicBookGroup.com

Canadian Cataloguing in Publication Data
Williams - Paquette, Bonnie
The B & B Cookbook
I. Cookery
II. Title Front Cover: Fruit Kabobs photograph by Laura Henderson
Produced by SIRCH Consulting
ISBN: 978-1-60860-973-4
Printed in the United States of America

Comments from some of our guests

"What can I say but … when can I move in? You two are absolutely awesome! What a gift you have and we are so grateful that you shared it with us. You feel like family, only better because you spoiled us rotten and who couldn't use a little of that?"

"As with our previous visits, this one was relaxing, enjoyable, and the ideal place to be while we are in Abbotsford. As you know, we consider you our B & B mentors and we still aspire to your standards—attention to detail, variety of foods, and wonderful service. Thanks for the inspiration."

"There are all kinds of people in the world; fortunately Don and Bonnie, you are people who take strangers into your world of peace and comfort and let them leave here feeling like family."

"This is one of the best B & B's I've been to, and I've been to quite a few. You have the warmest and friendliest personalities in this business and it shows, not just through yourself but your home. Thanks for having me. I'm definitely coming back."

"Thanks, B & D, for the robes, pillows once again, and for a more than comfortable—no, a luxurious—stay. From the suite, the foods, but most of all our hosts. Don't change a thing."

"Thanks so much for your generosity and hospitality. Jane and I enjoyed staying at your B & B with its ultimate comfort and location that was within distance to many."

"Thank you for welcoming us into your lovely home. We had a most enjoyable stay. Your recommendation for a round trip to Minter Gardens and along the river was a nice trip."

"We truly enjoyed our stay and your wonderful and warm hospitality with all the comforts of home. Thank you for having us as your guests."

Contents

Acknowledgements

I have to thank my wonderful husband, Don, who has listened to me for years about this book and finally made this quirky trip with me and helped at every turn. Thanks to two of our daughters, Kelly and Suzanne (named by age only), who are the only two children to see this book in its infancy; to our many wonderful guests who made me want to do this and, of course, to a guest-turned-B & B-owner-turned-editor who supported me in putting my ideas and recipes to paper and made it all look good, Gena Robertson. You came for a visit to see family and look what we ended up doing! Who knew? To Ric Pringle, who comes with Gena (significant other for the past thirty years) and had us laughing for days.

This book would not be complete if Laura Henderson and Jonathan Snyder from Offload Studios Photography had not been in our kitchen taking photos week after week, along with Matt (who helped eat what was cooked—you wouldn't believe what this lad can put away) and Bill Henderson, father of the lovely Laura.

I have to thank Martha Stewart for her long-running television series and magazine. I watched for years, and had a subscription for as many years. Thanks also to all the magazines on the market today that offer ideas, suggestions, and recipes and to the doctors offices where I may have borrowed a few recipes from time to time. Haven't we all? Be honest!

To the original Designer Guys, Steven and Chris, who gave us ideas for renovating in the early years, and my best decorator/friend in the world, Daryl Mytron, who brought this old lady into the 21st century with style and class (not me, the house).

I hope that, by reading this book and using the recipes, you will have as much fun and enjoyment in your lives as we have in ours.

Good B & B-ing! I maintain that if you follow what is suggested here, your guests will enter as strangers and leave as friends. They really will.

**Bonnie Williams-Paquette,
Owner Holly Arch Bed & Breakfast
Abbotsford, British Columbia, Canada**

Holly Arch Bed & Breakfast

Welcome

"… the pictures of your house on your website really caught our eye, and it is even more impressive in person."

Ten years ago, my husband and I decided to open a bed & breakfast. It was a natural extension of who we were. I loved to cook, as did my husband of twenty years, and we often lovingly prepared four-to nine-course dinners for family and friends. We'd share the creating and cooking, but I'd always do the baking. Homemade muffins, cakes, cookies, and scones, have always equated to family, comfort, and home to me.

A year before we opened our bed and breakfast, we spent time in the library to read all we could on the rules and regulations for Canadian, American, and European establishments to try to put it all together to come up with something a little unique. We sampled recipes for a year. Every Sunday we took turns trying different things and rating them. We had to quit and join Weight Watchers to undo the damage we caused ourselves. (It's true!)

When we first opened the B & B, we wondered if anyone would show up. Guess what? They did—often repeatedly. Over the years we have discovered what works and what doesn't in terms of the practical aspects of B & B-ing, what recipes bring accolades, and what personal touches mean the most. The thing is, it takes a little effort, imagination, and attention to detail, but it's not that hard!

Our B & B has brought us joy, and helped us through hard times. When my husband was ill with heart disease and I had cancer, the B & B was often what kept us focused and positive. The people we have met are amazing! They inspire us, and make us laugh and hopefully we inspire them and give them a home away from home that is the ultimate pampering experience.

This book will show you how to create that exceptional B & B and give you proven recipes your guests will love. With these recipes, hints and tips, your B & B can provide your guests with an experience they'll always remember.

Bonnie Williams–Paquette

To Be or Not To B & B
Making the Decision

While you are deciding whether to open a B & B, it would be a good idea to think about a few things. How many B & B's are in your area, town, or neighborhood? If you live in a city of about 150,000 people, then check it out. It may be that fifteen to twenty aren't too many. Can you carve yourself out a niche?

To operate a bed and breakfast, your area may have by-laws and zoning regulations with which you must comply. Also, licensing is important. If this is the case, an inspector will come out and check the B & B area, your home, yard, stairs, driveway, etc. to make sure it is within the regulations of your area and safe for your guests. You will have to consider if you can arrange your budget to cover any must-change items, such as a railing up the stairs to your front door.

Does your home lend itself to having guests? Is the room private? Do guests have their own bathroom? Not everyone wants to share a bathroom, so keep that in mind. Do you have room for, and can you accommodate, children? Do you really want to? If so, what ages? Do you have, or can you get, furnishings to accommodate an infant? If you can and are willing to do so, then be sure you advertise same.

Will someone be home all the time or part of the time? If not, you will need to arrange to have someone available for your guests. Are you comfortable with having total strangers in your home? You might want to consider getting a security system in your home. Some of them are not expensive to get installed and may ease your angst. We always think ahead to "what if" and are as prepared as we can be for any situation.

Do you have pets in your home? Are they well-behaved? You will need to keep them out of the B & B since some of your guests will have allergies to pet dander. Will you let your guests bring pets? If so, under what circumstances? In either case (you have pets or you'll allow them to visit) be sure and advertise clearly so people are aware.

Another point to consider is if the room is soundproof or on another side of the house from your bedroom. Is it a separate building from the main house? Is there enough parking? In our area, this is a big consideration. Will it interfere with your neighbors? Be sure and check. They may be nice and friendly, but if you were to put a business in your home, would the traffic or noise coming from within the confines of your property upset them?

To be a good B & B host, you have to like people, like dealing with people, and most of all, enjoy people from all walks of life, all religions, and all nationalities. This may sound like repetition, but it isn't. Are you able to work around the constraints of different religions or cultures? Be sure to ask yourself this and answer it honestly. Guests can tell and certainly feel if it is not what you advertise.

"This has simply been the most delightful experience of Canadian culture and its people for us—thanks to your warmth, kindness and unique hospitality. You have reinforced the belief that we have always held firm, there are no strangers in the world . . . only friends waiting to be met. You have a beautiful home, and most importantly, it is filled with love."

Renovating

You want to open a bed and breakfast that is exceptional—not just a bedroom down the hall with one bathroom which they have to share with you.

Guests need and want their own bathroom. It should have at least a shower, bath, or Jacuzzi tub, toilet, a sink, mirror, and good lighting. You may want to invest in new taps, new shower doors, or new flooring in the bathroom. Make sure it looks clean and modern.

Can you afford to put in new carpeting in the bedroom if the old one is stained and worn? Or perhaps replace it with new flooring? If your home is a little older and the paint could be looking a little fresher, then arrange to buy the paint and take time to redo the room or rooms. Make sure the base boards are looking clean and fresh and are not broken or missing. Keep the window sills free from dead flies and dust. Wash your curtains and iron them so you can almost smell cleanliness without offending someone with allergies.

Do you have a fireplace? Can you afford to put in an electric one? Is it needed? Try to think of what would help you feel relaxed and happy when you are away from home.

Have you ever heard of a bed and breakfast that didn't have a kitchen? We were in the middle of renovating our kitchen when the largest dog show in Canada was about to take place. Months before, we had booked one of the judges for the duration of the show. Did I have contact information for her? Of course not. I panicked and called a wonderful lady and friend, who was the manager of sales at one of our hotels and I asked for her help. The deal was every morning as our guest was leaving our home, I was to call the hotel restaurant and tell them she was on her way (she didn't have time to stand in line and wait for a table to become available). She ordered what she wanted and then we were to go down and pay for it. After her stay we went to the hotel to pay and they said it was already looked after as we had enough stress to deal with. How great is that?

Furnishing & Decorating

We offer our guests the very best we can afford. It took us ten years of always upgrading until we got it right.

The bed is very important. It should be comfortable and attractive. The chairs, tables, and other furnishings should complement each other in terms of style and colour. If you can, put a small fridge in the space so guests can keep water, drinks, or snacks cold. Make sure they have closet space to hang their clothes, and good hangers. Have drawers where they can lay out their personal belongings.

Hang appropriate pictures that suit the character of the home. Try and run the same theme through the house to give consistency. This all takes time and effort on your part but is so worth it when completed.

Back to the bed. We use only 650-thread count sheets and pillow cases. The feeling is incredibly sensuous for people of all ages; try to get the most luxurious duvets and pillows. You can buy these on sale. We bought ours at a price that was less than 250 thread count was selling for. Always have on hand extra pillows, blankets, and throw blankets that can be used for an afternoon nap. Add to this mix the fluffiest towels your budget can handle. You can get really good towels at department stores and discount malls. You can tell by the feel if it is luxurious or not. If you

can, ask family to get them for you for Christmas (I have done this).

" ... as a bed & breakfast, I just wanted to pass on our bouquet of appreciation for the warm, and inviting hospitality shown to us by our hosts, Bonnie and Don. They made us feel right at home in the upstairs suite and the duvet comforter and mattress was like sleeping on a cloud. Our meals were elegantly presented and equally delicious. Everything to the littlest details with style and elegance

I would highly recommend the Holly Arch Bed and Breakfast to visitors and tourists to the region and to local residents for a stay of TLC in every detail ... "

Buy soaps, lotions, unscented candles. Again, buy them in outlet malls or buy them when they are on sale. When we were on holiday we were in an outlet mall and they had a buy three, get two for free sale. I bought soaps, hand soaps, body lotions, and hand lotions all in the same scent and I have

enough to last at least two years. That was a good investment. Using the same philosophy as with linens, purchase three-ply toilet paper and Kleenex. The details mean a lot.

Keep a drawer filled with items your guests may-have forgotten, such as toothpaste, toothbrushes shower caps, sewing kit, shaving lotion, hand lotion, bath oils, body washes, disposable razors, shampoo, and conditioner. You will be complimented over and over again because you paid attention to details and these items add to the comfort of your guest. Also, have on hand a hair dryer just for the B & B guest.

Bathrobes—here again, buy the softest, fluffiest you can find and afford. We had ours monogrammed by a local company in our colors. We hang them in the bathroom.

Have an area with brochures, menus of local restaurants, tours that can be taken, places to see.

Make it the information centre. If you have coupons for dining establishments, be sure to offer them to your guests. Keep magazines, books, and appropriate movies at the ready.

We also have a large map of the world framed on the wall. Guests are invited to put a pin in it to mark where they are from. It's fun for the guests and starts conversations.

If the guest facilities are upstairs in your home, you might have to ask your guests not to wear shoes upstairs. Have a basket at the bottom of the stairs filled with slippers for your guests to wear.

"We have traveled many countries of the world. Some of our houses and hotels have been average, some good, some very good—rarely excellent. Truly we can say that Holly Arch is none of these—it is as close to perfection as it is possible to be. Thank you both so very much, especially as our being in Abbotsford has been sad and frustrating. In two days you have become friends and practical support for us. May God bless you both—real good."

Putting in Your Own Special Touches

You want your B & B to be unique. Part of this is getting the furnishings, decorations, and food right. Part of it is using your own talents, skills, interests, and personality to make the place special. If you're an artist, hang one of your paintings. If you collect antiques, put some in the B & B. If you love poetry, put your favourite book of poetry by the bed. If you love to hike, you could put some photos of your favourite trails. Maybe you have a friend who is a talented blacksmith, or who makes wicker baskets or does calligraphy. Think of what you could do to bring your own special touches to the B & B.

We give Canadian flag lapel pins to all out-of-country visitors. We ask them to take a little of Canada home with them. Is there something in your area that you are particularly proud of? Maybe you could send your guests home with a memento.

Outside the Bed and Breakfast

First impressions happen only once, so it is up to you as the bed and breakfast owner, to make sure the grass is cut, weeds are pulled, and everything has been watered (following the by-laws of your area in the summer). If you have a large property and can afford a gardener once a week, perhaps this is possible. If you can only afford it once a month but are able to keep it looking great the rest of the time, be sure to keep on top of it. If you have to do it yourself, look at the positive side—you are getting exercise.

Make sure the siding on your home has been power washed and is clean and that there is no paint peeling. Can you create a focal point in the yard, be it a pond or flower bed—something that catches the eye and draws you closer? The porch/entry of your home should be clear of clutter, and the glass in the doors should be clean.

Keep all toys and bikes off the driveway so your guests may park their vehicle and walk without fear of falling. If you have pets, such as dogs, make really sure they are trained not to jump up on strangers. They should be well behaved or out of the way. We do not have pets and we ask that you leave your beloved pet behind. It is hard having to refuse guests their request and then lose them as customers. As I mentioned, the main reason is allergies—other people's, not ours.

If you don't have a private balcony for your guests can you find a private space for them to sit outside and relax? A well thought-out space, inside and out, will reward you and your guests again and again.

Most people do not smoke anymore. If you do, please be sure to do so outside and away from your room(s). I know this is hard, but if you are near an outside door, just close it so the smoke doesn't get into the room. We appreciate this and so will future guests.

Getting the Word Out and Guests In

Our guests have come from South Africa, West Africa, Australia, New Zealand, Russia, Spain, England, Scotland, France, all the Scandinavian countries, from all across Canada, and the U.S.A. They have been doctors, pilots, newly-weds, single girls or guys, retirees, and families. The occasions have been just as varied; some are here on vacations and adventures, some here to meet with sick relatives, or get some space away from children. Some celebrate weddings, anniversaries or other special occasions (Valentine's Day is a big one). So how did they learn about us?

One of the best methods to get the word out about your B & B is the Internet. Set up a website and join the National B & B site. Also, if your local tourism association has a magazine for travelers, get an ad in it. Join the local Chamber of Commerce. Invite the members of the tourism association to come for breakfast and serve them the very same fare you would serve your guests. (It is not a good idea to try to show a creation your guests will never see). We have done this with the tourism association here every year since we opened. It allows them to see what we have to offer and what our guests will dine on when they are here. As new staff come and go each year, it is to our benefit to do this.

Make sure that your marketing materials, ads, website, etc. give the impression you want to convey—quality, exceptionality. Use branding. Decide on what colours, logos, fonts, and style you want. Stick to it so people see your materials and instantly know they are from your B & B. You might want to send a newsletter to your guests once you have established yourself. You need to adhere to the privacy legislation.

Try cross-marketing. Is there an exceptional restaurant in your area? Perhaps they will put your brochures or cards in their restaurant if you put theirs in your B & B. Are there events, courses, attractions that people come to your area to attend? If so, be sure to introduce yourselves to those people and ensure they know about your B & B.

Remember, you market yourself everywhere you go, and every time you answer the phone, or an email. The impressions they receive about you are important. When answering the phone or sending an email, be friendly and approachable, but convey professionalism.

We Have Guests!

When your guests book, be sure to confirm the price, time and date of their arrival, and details of their departure. Write down contact information and be sure to ask if there are any food restriction, allergies, or food they do not want to see on their plate. We always ask for one night deposit when they make the reservation (others ask for a 50 percent down payment). The day the guests are coming, do a check one more time to make sure the bathroom is spotless, the bedroom as well, being sure to leave a chocolate on the pillow (just like the big guys!) If there is a third room, that the television screen is clean and everything looks in order.

Greet them at the door with a big smile and warm handshake. If your health allows, please help carry in the luggage. Think about whether you will offer a tray of fruit, cheese, cold or hot beverage when they first arrive. Take the time to have a little chit chat, then take them on a tour of the B & B. Show them where they will eat and give them a choice of times for breakfast. Give them a house key. Show them where the fire extinguishers are, any quirky things about the house (like if the taps are on backwards like ours). Let them know about any rules or restrictions you have (like no, they can't bring the dog downstairs). If they smoke, ask them to smoke outside and away from an open door or window. Most smokers know this before

hand, but be sure to remind them so there are no problems. Do you expect your guests to stay outside if you are not at home? Can they come and go as they please? Be sure there are no surprises and your guests know what to expect and what you expect.

Will you want to have coffee ready for your guests to enjoy while they are getting ready for breakfast? Will you take a tray to them? Will you offer them to come and help themselves? These are things that will crop up and you have to know what you want to do.

We consider ourselves ambassadors of our fair city, which is surrounded by beautiful mountains, scenic valleys, and lakes, and world-class gardens. We are close to mini golf, regular golf, tennis, swimming, skiing, and hiking and we will suggest, when asked, for places to go and sights to see.

We are proud to say in all the years we have been doing this, there has not been one person that we would not welcome back into our home. We treat everyone that crosses our doorway the way we would hope to be treated. Friendly, but not nosy, and never rudely. We are available for our guests and are willing to assist whenever asked.

We have had a few mishaps in ten years, but they have been funny. We had one lady who came down in the middle of the night and set off the alarms. Poor thing almost had a heart attack (I know I did). She said she didn't realize that it would go off.

Another was a sweet lady who was rushing to leave and broke her shoelace. I found one (I didn't even think we had any) and it was even the right color. I felt positively brilliant and she thinks I was some kind of hero.

"Bonnie's firm handshake and warm welcome and Don's relaxed friendliness are special memories that don't translate easily to guest book or evaluation form, but will stay with me when I think of our last minutes together. Elderly arthritic guest comes down the stairs to be met by hostess with glass of water and guests forgotten pills. Husband stands by, ready to take guest to the airport. She ties her shoes and promptly breaks a shoelace. Now what? Hostess sweeps off and returns with the needed black round shoelace, correct length. Who can beat that?"

Have your recipes and table settings chosen ahead of time to reduce stress. Our longest guest stayed twenty-one days and, believe it or not, nothing was duplicated. Settings, food . . . we have over a thousand recipes to choose from, so I guess getting prepared before opening for business was a good idea. We keep all menus on the computer in case they make a return visit and we won't have to present them with the same breakfast they had before, unless of course they request it.

We also keep a card in a recipe box holder showing the date, who, what, and where the recipe came from. This was something I learned from Martha Stewart years ago and was one of the best ideas I clung to.

We also give our guests a thank-you letter asking them to tell their friends if they enjoyed their stay; to tell the tourism association if we exceeded their expectations, and to please tell us if something should be changed. Getting suggestions are great.

Breakfast

What Makes it Exceptional?

I have a story to tell you. A few years ago we were in Montreal and the bed & breakfast we stayed at microwaved everything: stale croissants, stale hot cross buns (four months after Easter), frozen waffles, and yes, vegetable pie in pastry (pastry that has been nuked is indescribable). The third day we went to McDonald's for breakfast. (This is a true story!)

Great food makes the difference between so-so and exceptional. The recipes I'm going to give you are not difficult, and they are proven to elicit more than one "wow!"

A beautiful table also makes the food taste even better. Beautiful place mats or a crisp, ironed tablecloth sets the mood, with matching cloth napkins and napkin rings. Dishes for the B & B should be exclusively for the B & B (not family). The same goes for silverware, glassware, and tablecloths. Buy the best you can, and don't be afraid to mix and match.

I used to set a special typed menu on the table each morning for our guests. Each new guest got a different menu; there is no set pattern that we use. Most of them took them as souvenirs for years, but last year, we found they were just left on the table. Now I just tell them as we present each course what it is they are getting. I guess it is more personal, although I liked the menu. Each day was different and each table setting was too!

Exceptional Recipes -Smoothies

One of the best things to make for breakfast is smoothies.

Nut and Chocolate Delight

Serves 2

2 bananas

3 tbsp peanut butter (smooth)

5 tbsp vanilla yogurt

2 scoops chocolate ice cream (good brand)

1 cup milk

¼ cup whipping cream

Chopped salted peanuts for garnish

Place peeled bananas in blender. Add peanut butter, yogurt, ice cream, and milk. Process until smooth. Add whipping cream and blend for a couple of seconds. Pour into chilled glasses, top with peanuts, and add a small straw. Serve immediately.

Nectarine Melt

This is really special with the use of lemon sorbet.

Serves 2

1 cup milk

2 cups lemon sorbet

1 ripe mango, pitted and diced

2 ripe nectarines, pitted and diced

Pour milk into blender; add one half of the sorbet and process gently until combined. Add remaining sorbet and process until smooth. When this is entirely blended, add the mango and nectarines and process until smooth. You can add a dollop of whipped cream on top. Pour in a tall glass, add short straws, and serve immediately.

If our guests are celebrating an anniversary or birthday, one of the prettiest smoothies is this one:

Pink Sky

Wonderfully fragrant, yet illusive flavour.

Serves 2

½ cup natural yogurt
½ cup milk
1 ½ cups whipping cream
1 tbsp. rose water
3 tbsp. honey
1 ripe mango, pitted and diced
6 ice cubes
edible rose petals (optional)

Pour yogurt, milk, and whipping cream into food processor or blender and process gently until combined. Add rose water and process until thoroughly blended, then add mango along with the ice cubes and process until smooth. Pour into chilled, fancy glasses. Decorate with the rose petals if you want to raise the bar to elegant.

Love's Blush

Serves 2

6 oz. cooked beets, chopped (yes, really!)
½ cup orange juice, chilled
5 tbsp. plain yogurt, chilled
⅓ cup mineral water, chilled (not fizzy)
½ cup whipping cream
touch of honey
Orange slices for decoration

First, puree the beets until smooth, then put all ingredients, except orange slices, in a blender and process until smooth. Pour into chilled glasses and decorate with orange slices. Use blood oranges if they are in season.

Maui Marvel

This will give you a much-needed energy boost

Serves 2

1 cup milk

3 ½ tbsp coconut milk

¾ cup vanilla ice cream

2 frozen bananas

1 cup canned pineapple chunks, drained (save juice)

1 sliced papaya, seeded and diced

Pour milk and coconut milk into a blender and process gently until mixed. Add half the ice cream and process gently until smooth. Add frozen banana slices and process well. Now add all the fruit and process until smooth. Dip glass rims in pineapple juice and then into sugar to coat the rim. Yummy!

Kiwi Dream

*Sweet, but with a sharper flavour—
very refreshing!*

Serves 2

⅔ cups milk

Juice of two limes

2 kiwi fruit, peeled and chopped

1 tbsp. sugar

2 cups vanilla premium ice cream

Strips of lime peel

Pour milk and lime juice in a blender and process until combined. Add fruit and sugar and process gently.Add ice cream and process until smooth. Pour into stemmed glasses and gently place lime strips on top. Serve immediately.

Exceptional Recipes -Fruit

This can be a simple bowl of strawberries and cream, or a fruit bowl or, what is even nicer—a fruit plate. We were at a bed and breakfast in Quebec and the host had thinly sliced kiwi, nectarine, strawberries, a small bunch of grapes and plated them beautifully. It was exceptional.

Many of our guests have not had the opportunity to try fruits from our part of the world—or at least ones we use that would be unusual or exceptional. You might try persimmons, peaches, nectarines, guava, or fresh figs (if you can find them—we have to drive into Vancouver to buy them and they are truly wonderful), grapes (red, purple, green), watermelon (red seedless, or yellow - yellow is fantastic and most people have never tasted it), cantaloupe, many different melons, plums, (red, black) and all the berries.

The best thing about fruit is you can make parfaits, bowls, plates or kabob; cook them, freeze them or eat them as they come naturally. For a fruit bowl, slice and cut fruit into different shapes (balls, triangles, squares), drizzle with honey. Fold into one cup sweetened whipped cream. Put into a fancy bowl and serve.

Ambrosia

Serves 2

¼ cup chopped pecans
¾ cup sweetened whipped cream
¼ cup chopped maraschino cherries
14 oz. can condensed milk
½ can (11 oz) mandarin slices
½ cup plain yogurt
½ cup mini marshmallows
¼ cup lime juice
3–4 oz. flaked coconut
½ (20 oz. can) pineapple tidbits, drained

Mix all the ingredients together and refrigerate for two to three hours before serving in pretty glass bowls. Garnish with some reserved orange slices. You can use blood oranges, if in season, for a colourful garnish.

Breakfast Parfait

Serves 2

Fresh blueberries
Granola
½–1 cup yogurt (vanilla or blueberry is best)
Raspberries
Warm honey

In tall glasses, place a generous spoonful of blueberries on the bottom, then place a granola layer on top (be generous here). Add yogurt (depending on size of dish). Add a layer of fresh raspberries and drizzle warm honey on top. Use two different melons for a different taste. Just make sure the melons are truly ripe. Pick a glass with a pretty shape for best results.

GRReat Grapefruit

Serves 2

1 pink grapefruit
1 tsp. vodka, to taste
2 tbsp. sour cream
2 tbsp. brown sugar

Cut grapefruit in half, then with a fruit knife run it between the membranes and around the outer edge to loosen the segments. Leave the segments in and try to keep juices in. Put a tsp. of vodka on top of each half and add a heaping tbsp. of sour cream on top and finish with a tbsp. of brown sugar. Place under the broiler until it bubbles. This is YUMMY.

Always ask your guests if they are taking cholesterol medication since grapefruit may be restricted from their diet.

Kabobs

Serves 2

For Kabobs use whatever you like: pineapple chunks, strawberries, kiwi, peaches, nectarines, and plums. Have on hand the following:

Six to eight wooden skewers
½ cup yogurt
1 tsp. honey
½ tsp. freshly grated nutmeg
2 tsp. lime juice
1 lime, thinly sliced

Prepare fruit into balls or chunks and thread onto skewers, using two skewers per person arrange across a plate. Combine all the ingredients and drizzle over kabob. Garnish with lime slices. If you wish, sprinkle with coconut.

When preparing this course for breakfast, be it for spouse, family, friends or company, try using different fruit. We are fortunate in this country to have such a selection it is a shame we don't use them as much as we can. Besides, how healthy can one get?

Kabobs

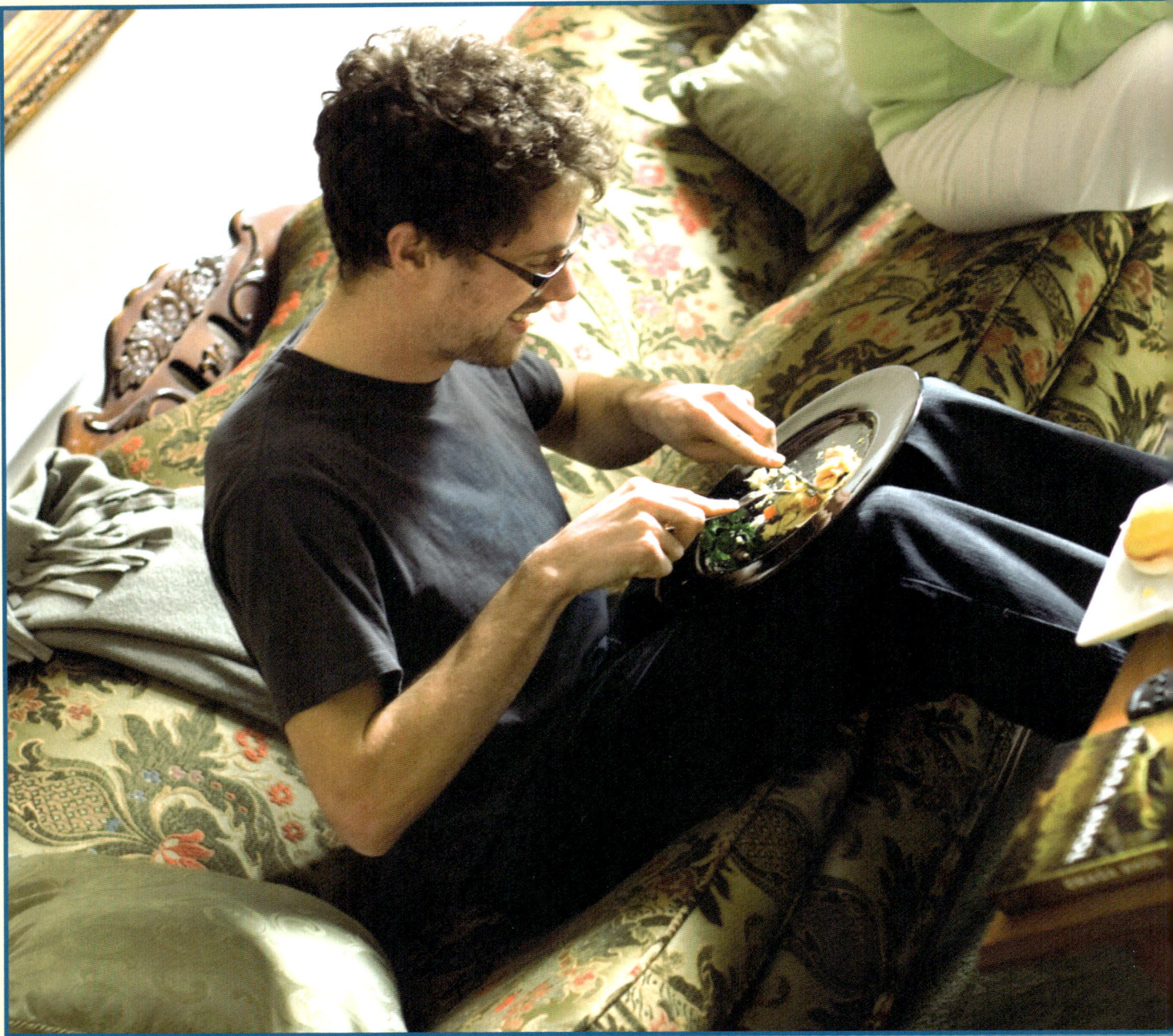

#1 food taster on photo shoot

Exceptional Recipes - Muffins, Scones, Bread

After the smoothie, present warm muffins with sweet butter to be eaten with a fruit plate or fruit bowl

"The breakfast feast was a monumental moment of epic proportion. The harmony of color, smell, composition, and taste provided complete sensory satisfaction. Beside the discomfort of overeating, the only issue was my lack of ability to reproduce such a breakfast at home—that is, until now!"

Love always, Matt Vogt

Apple Cinnamon Muffins

2 cups flour
½ cup white sugar
3 tsp. baking power
½ tsp. cinnamon
¼ tsp. salt
½ cup butter
½ cup chopped pecans

1 egg
⅔ cup milk
1 tsp. cinnamon
1 tbsp. brown sugar
1 large Granny Smith apple,
peeled and diced

Makes 6

Preheat oven to 425 degrees. Sift flour, sugar, baking powder, cinnamon, and salt in a medium-sized bowl. Cut up butter with a pastry blender. Measure out ½ cup and reserve for the topping. Add the apple and pecans to the mix. Beat the egg and add the milk. Pour into the dry mixture and stir until just mixed (this will be lumpy). Spoon into greased muffin tins about ¾ full. Mix together cinnamon and sugar and sprinkle over each muffin. Bake for fifteen to twenty minutes.

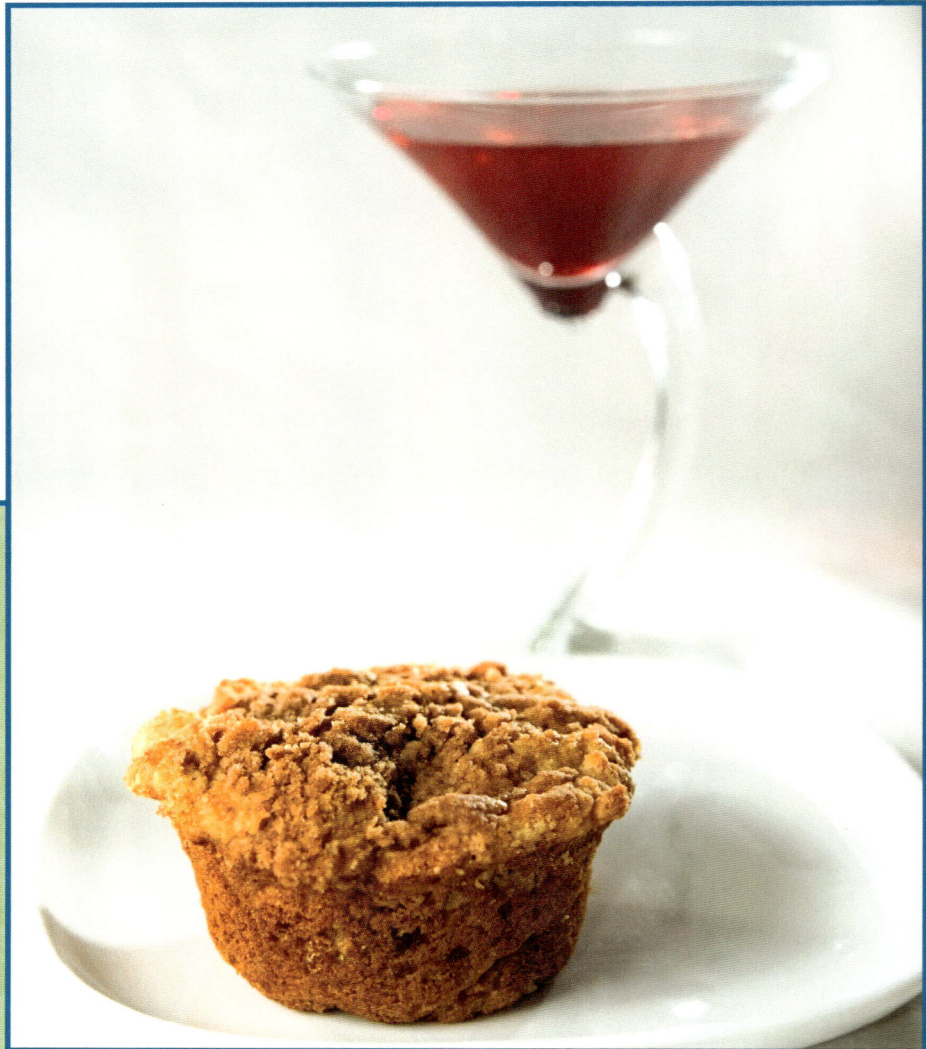

Apple Streusel Muffin with Glass of Pomegranite Juice

Apple Streusel Muffins

Makes 6

2 cups flour
1 cup sugar
1 tsp. baking powder
½ tsp. baking soda
Pinch of salt
2 eggs
½ cup butter, melted
1 ¼ tsp. vanilla extract
1 ½ cups chopped, peeled Granny Smith apples

Streusel Topping

⅓ cup packed brown sugar
1 tbsp. flour
⅛ tsp. ground cinnamon
1 tbsp. cold butter

Glaze

1 ½ cups icing sugar
1–2 tbsp. cream
1 tsp. melted butter
¼ tsp. vanilla
⅛ tsp. salt

Preheat oven to 375 degrees.
In a bowl, combine flour, sugar, baking powder, baking soda, and salt. In another bowl, whisk eggs, butter, and vanilla, then stir into dry ingredients just until moistened (batter will be stiff). Fold in apples. Fill greased muffin cups ¾ full. In a small bowl, combine streusel topping ingredients, cutting in butter until crumbly. Sprinkle over muffins.
Bake for fifteen to twenty minutes, or until toothpick comes out clean. Cool for five minutes before removing to rack to cool. Combine glaze ingredients and drizzle over muffins.

Blueberry Stuffed Muffins

2 cups flour
½ cup sugar
3 tsp. baking powder
½ tsp. salt
Rind of one lemon

1 large egg
1 cup milk
½ cup melted butter
1 cup blueberries (fresh or frozen)
Lemon curd (recipe page 20)

Makes 6

Preheat oven to 425 degrees.
Mix flour, sugar, baking powder, salt, and lemon rind in a medium bowl and set aside. Beat egg, then add milk and butter in a two-cup measuring bowl. Add wet mixture to dry ingredients, stirring just until mixed. (Batter will appear lumpy.) Stir in blueberries and fill muffin tins ½ full, add a teaspoon of lemon curd in the center of each muffin, and cover with the remaining batter. Bake for twenty minutes.

Topping

½ cup melted butter
1 tbsp. lemon juice
½ cup white sugar

Combine butter and lemon juice in a bowl. Put sugar in another bowl. Dunk the tops of the muffins, first in the butter and then the sugar.
Or
Set the hot muffins on a cooling rack on a cookie sheet. Cover the muffin tops with icing or cream cheese icing and let it melt. Remove from rack and serve these warm. This is my favourite way to enjoy them.

Cheese and Bacon Muffins

Absolutely terrific when served with scrambled eggs

Makes 6

8 strips bacon, reserving drippings
1 ½ cups flour
½ cup cornmeal
1 tbsp. baking powder
½ tsp. salt
2 cups grated Balderson's
Cheddar Cheese
3 tbsp. melted butter
3 tbsp. bacon drippings
1 large egg
1 cup milk
½ cup coarsely grated Balderson's
Cheddar Cheese for topping

Preheat oven to 425 degrees. Cook and drain bacon, reserving the drippings. When cool, crumble the bacon. Combine the first six ingredients. Melt the butter and add to the reserved drippings. In a medium bowl, beat the egg lightly, milk and add to the butter/bacon mixture. Now add this to the dry ingredients and stir thoroughly. Fill muffin tins ¾ full and sprinkle cheese on top. Bake for twenty minutes.

Banana White Chocolate Muffins

Makes 6

1 large egg
¼ cup Crisco oil
4 pureed bananas
½ cup milk
2 cups flour
¼ cup sugar
2 tbsp. baking powder
⅓ cup grated white chocolate
⅓ cup ground pecans

Preheat oven to 400 degrees. In a bowl, blend eggs, oil, bananas, and milk. In another bowl mix the flour, sugar, baking powder, white chocolate, and pecans. Make a well in the centre of the dry ingredients and add the milk mixture. Stir only until moistened. Fill greased muffins tins ¾ full. Bake fifteen to twenty minutes or until they turn a light golden colour.

Cheesecake Muffins

Gluten-free diets where milk products can be tolerated

Makes 6

3 (8-ounce) packages cream cheese
1 cup white sugar
5 eggs
1 tsp. pure vanilla extract

Sour Cream Topping
8 ounces sour cream
1 cup white sugar
1 tsp. pure vanilla extract

Preheat oven to 350 degrees and line muffin tins with liners (yes, here you have to).

In a medium bowl, cream together the cream cheese and one cup sugar. Stir in the eggs one at a time then add the vanilla. Spoon into the cupcake holders to about ¾ full.
To make the sour cream topping whisk together the sour cream, one cup sugar and vanilla until smooth. Spoon into the center of each muffin.
Bake for thirty minutes in the oven until golden brown. Remove from oven and cool for five to ten minutes. Return it to the oven and bake for an additional seven minutes until set. Place pans on racks to cool. DO NOT remove from the pan until they are completely cool.

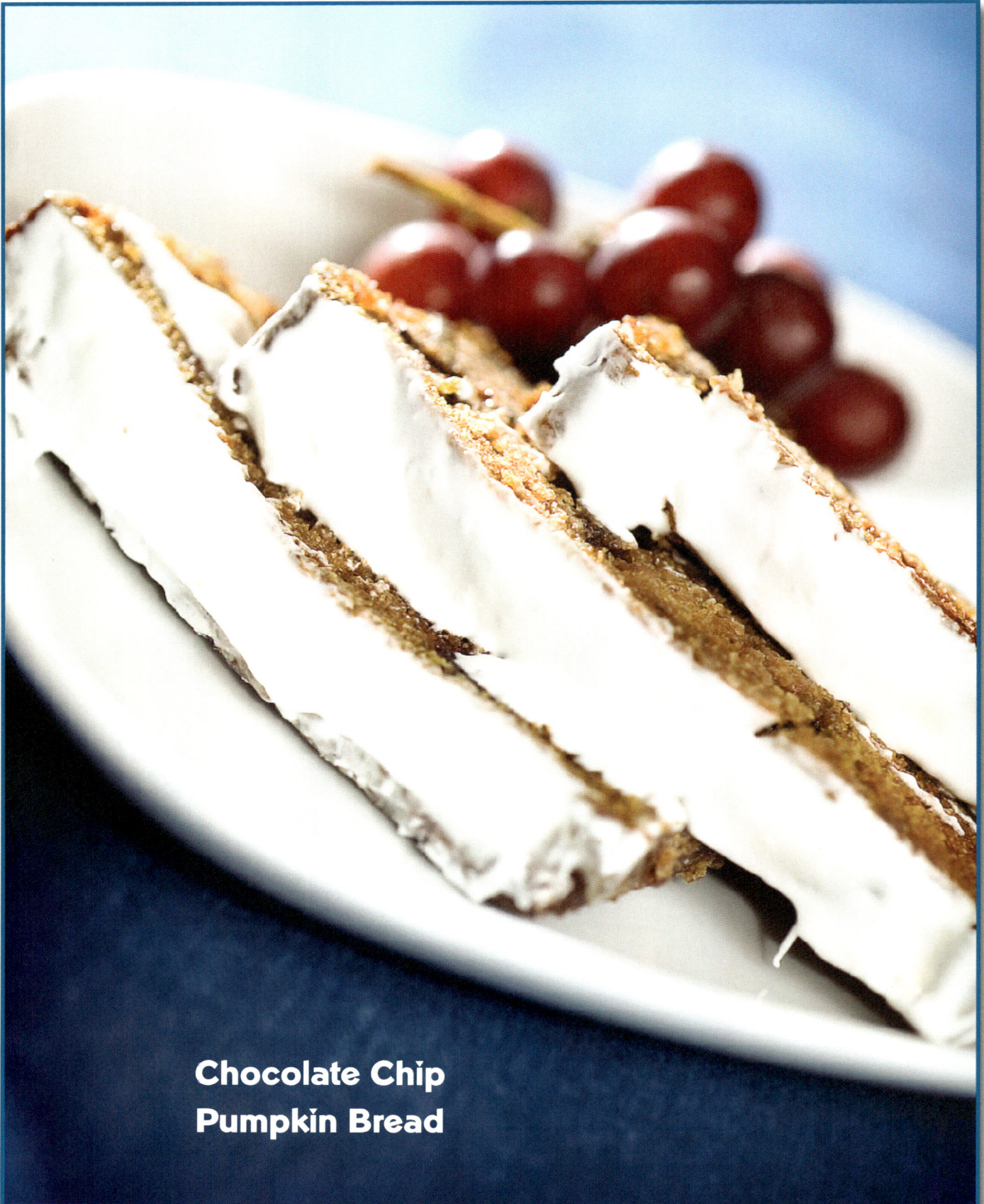

Chocolate Chip Pumpkin Bread

Chocolate Chip Pumpkin Bread

Makes three loaves

3 cups white sugar
1 (15 oz.) canned pure
pumpkin
1 cup Crisco oil
⅔ cup water
4 eggs
3 ½ cups flour
1 tbsp. ground
cinnamon

1 tbsp. ground nutmeg
2 tsp. baking soda
1 ½ tsp. salt
1 cup semi-sweet
chocolate chips
½ cups pecans

Preheat oven 350 degrees. Grease and flour three 9 x 5 inch loaf pans. In a large bowl, combine sugar, pumpkin, oil, water, and eggs. Beat until smooth. Blend in flour, cinnamon, nutmeg, baking soda, and salt. Fold in chocolate chips and nuts. Fill loaf pans ½ to ¾ full.

Bake for one hour or until the knife comes out clean. Cool on wire racks before removing from pans.

Chocolate Cinnamon Rolls

¾ tsp. quick-rising yeast
1 tbsp. warm water (approx. 110 degrees)
1 ⅛ cups of flour
2 tbsp. white sugar, divided
¼ tsp. salt
3 tbsp. cold butter, divided
¼ cup warm milk (again, 110 degrees)
1 egg yolk
2 tbsp. brown sugar
¼ tsp. ground cinnamon
⅓ cup miniature chocolate chips

Glaze
⅓ cup icing sugar
1 ½ tsp. butter
¼ tsp. pure vanilla extract
1 ½ tsp. hot water

In a small bowl, dissolve the yeast in the water and set aside. In a bowl, combine flour, 1 tbsp. white sugar and salt. Cut in the 2 tbsp. butter until crumbly. Add the milk, egg yolk, and yeast mixture, stirring well. Cover with plastic wrap and keep in fridge overnight. Turn dough onto a lightly floured surface. Roll out into a 10 x 6 inch rectangle. Melt remaining butter. Brush butter on the dough to within ½ inch of the edge. Combine the brown sugar, cinnamon and remaining white sugar. Sprinkle over the dough, then sprinkle the chocolate chips on top. Roll up, starting with the short edge, and pinch the seam to seal. Cut into one-inch slices. Place cut side down in a well greased 8-inch square pan. Cover and allow to rise until doubled, approximately ninety minutes.

Preheat oven to 375 degrees. Bake for sixteen to eighteen minutes until golden. In a small bowl, mix the glaze ingredients and drizzle over the still-warm rolls. Serve immediately.

Cinnamon Apple Puff

1 very large Granny Smith apple
(peeled, cored and sliced thin)
3 tbsp. butter
3 eggs
½ cup flour
½ cup whole milk
1 tsp. sugar
Dash of salt
2 tbsp. cinnamon sugar
Juice of a whole lemon

Preheat oven to 475 degrees. Grease 9" quiche dish well. Sauté apple in 1 tbsp. butter until slightly tender. Spread slices evenly in quiche dish. Mix together eggs, flour, milk, sugar, and salt until well blended. Now pour over apple slices and bake ten minutes. Dot with remaining butter and sprinkle with cinnamon sugar. Return to oven for about five minutes. Bring to the table puffed and sprinkle with lemon juice.

(Above) Nut and Chocolate Smoothie with Cranberry Pecan Scones

Cinnamon, Pecan, and Cranberry Cream Scones

Makes 6 wedges

¼ cup heavy cream, plus extra for brushing scones
1 large egg yolk
½ tsp vanilla
1 cup flour
3 tbsp. sugar plus extra for sprinkling on scones
¼ tsp. salt

1 ½ tsp. baking powder
¼ tsp. baking soda
½ tsp. cinnamon
3 tbsp. cold butter, cut into bits
¼ cup chopped pecans
¼ cup dried cranberries

Preheat oven to 400 degrees. In a small bowl, whisk together ¼ cup of the cream, egg yolk, and vanilla. Into a bowl sift together the flour, 3 tbsp. sugar, salt, baking powder, baking soda, and cinnamon. Add the butter and cut in until mixture resembles coarse meal. Stir in the pecans and cranberries. Add the cream mixture and stir with a fork until the mixture forms a sticky, but manageable dough. Knead the dough on a lightly floured surface for about thirty seconds; pat into a ¾ inch thick round and cut into six wedges. Transfer the wedges to a parchment paper lined baking sheet. Brush them with the additional cream and sprinkle with sugar. Bake scones in the middle of a preheated oven for fifteen to eighteen minutes, or until golden.

Cranberry Apple Bread

Cranberry Apple Bread

Makes one loaf

2 cups peeled and chopped
Granny Smith Apples
¾ cup white sugar
2 tbsp. Crisco Oil
1 egg
1 ½ cups flour
1 ½ tsp. baking powder
½ tsp. baking soda
1 tsp. ground cinnamon
1 cup fresh or frozen cranberries
½ cup chopped pecans

Preheat oven to 350 degrees. Lightly grease 9 x 5 inch loaf pan. Stir together apples, sugar and oil. Add egg and mix well. Sift together dry ingredients. Now stir the dry ingredients into the wet, mixing only until moist. Stir in cranberries and pecans. Spoon batter into loaf pan.
Bake thirty-five to forty minutes until toothpick inserted in the center of the loaf comes out clean. This can be served warm. To keep, wrap in plastic wrap and then tin foil and freeze.

French Breakfast Puffs

Makes 6

1 ½ cups flour
½ cup sugar
1 ½ tsp. baking powder
¼ tsp. ground nutmeg
Pinch salt
1 egg
½ cup milk
⅓ cup melted butter
¼ cup sugar
½ tsp. ground cinnamon
¼ cup melted butter

Preheat oven to 350 degrees. In a mixing bowl, combine first five ingredients and make a well in center. In another bowl, beat egg slightly, add milk and melted butter. Mix together well and add to dry ingredients. Stir only until moistened (will be lumpy). Grease muffin tins; fill full with batter. Bake twenty to twenty-five minutes or until golden.
Combine ¼ cup sugar and cinnamon together. Immediately dip muffins into the melted butter and then into the sugar-cinnamon mix. Serve warm. This is a real winner.

Gingerbread Muffins with Homemade Lemon Curd

Lemon Curd
⅔ cup sugar
¾ tsp. cornstarch
⅓ cup lemon juice
5 egg yolks, lightly beaten
¼ cup butter, cut into pieces
2 tsp. grated fresh lemon peel

Muffins
2 cups flour
¼ cup sugar
2 ½ tsp. baking powder
2 tsp. ground ginger
1 tsp. ground cinnamon
Pinch of salt
¼ tsp. ground cloves
1 egg
¾ cups milk
¼ cup Crisco oil
¼ cup molasses

Makes 6

Preheat oven to 375 degrees. In a heavy saucepan, whisk sugar, cornstarch, and lemon juice until smooth. Bring to a boil and stir for two minutes or until slightly thickened. Stir a small amount into egg yolks and return this into saucepan. Bring to a boil and, stirring constantly, cook another two minutes until mixture reaches 160 degrees and coats the back of a spoon.

Remove from heat; gently stir in butter and lemon peel until blended. Pour into a bowl and cover with plastic wrap, ensuring plastic wrap touches the entire surface. Place in fridge until ready to serve.

In a bowl, combine flour, sugar, baking powder, ginger, cinnamon, salt, and cloves. In another bowl whisk egg, milk, oil, and molasses until smooth; stir in dry ingredients just until moistened.

Fill muffin tins half full and bake for fifteen to twenty minutes. Cool five minutes before removing to a wire rack. Serve warm with lemon curd. Wait for the accolades.

Homemade Cinnamon Buns

Makes 12

1 cup warm milk
(approx. 110 degrees)
2 eggs at room temperature
⅓ cup melted butter
4 ½ cups flour
1 tsp. salt
½ cup white sugar
2 ½ tsp. quick-rising yeast
1 cup brown sugar, packed
2½ tbsp. ground cinnamon
⅓ cup butter, softened
1 (3-oz). package of
softened cream cheese
¼ cup softened butter
1½ cups icing sugar
½ tsp. pure vanilla extract
⅛ tsp. salt

Place ingredients in the bread machine in the order recommended by the manufacturer. Select dough cycle and press start.

After the dough has doubled in size turn it out on a lightly floured surface, cover and let rest for about ten minutes. In a small bowl, combine the brown sugar and cinnamon.

Roll dough to a 16 x 21 inch (approx.) rectangle. Spread dough with ⅓ cup softened butter and sprinkle evenly with the brown sugar/cinnamon mixture. Roll up and cut into twelve buns. Place buns in a lightly greased 9 x 13 inch baking pan. Cover and allow to rise until nearly doubled, about thirty minutes.

Preheat oven to 400 degrees. Bake buns until golden brown, about fifteen minutes. While buns are baking, beat together the cream cheese, ¼ cup butter, icing sugar, vanilla, and salt.

Spread frosting on warm rolls before plating and serving. Guests will probably tell you they taste just like the ones in the mall. When they do, just smile!

"These are honestly the best cinnamon buns I have ever had."

–Jonathan Snyder

Phantom Spring Rhubarb Muffins

These will not keep … hence the name. Sooooooo good!

Makes 12

½ cup sour cream
¼ cup Crisco Oil
1 large egg
1⅓ cups flour
1 cup diced rhubarb
⅔ cup brown sugar
½ tsp. baking soda
Pinch of salt

Preheat oven to 350 degrees. Blend together sour cream, oil, and egg. Set aside. In another bowl, mix the next five ingredients together and then combine with the first mixture. Mix only until just moistened. Fill twelve large muffin tins about ⅔ full.

Topping
¼ cup packed brown sugar
¼ cup chopped pecans
½ tsp. cinnamon
2 tsp. melted butter

Combine ingredients and spoon onto each muffin. Bake for about thirty minutes.

Raspberry Cream Cheese Muffins

Makes 6

1 ¾ cups flour
1 tsp. baking powder
½ tsp. baking soda
¼ tsp. salt
½ cup melted butter
1 pkg. cream cheese (8 oz)
2 large eggs
¼ cup light cream
1 tsp. vanilla
¼ cup raspberry jam (seedless)
¼ cup softened butter
¼ cup flour
¼ cup packed brown sugar
1 tsp. cinnamon

Preheat oven to 350 degrees. Grease muffin tin. In a large bowl combine first four ingredients. In another bowl cream the butter, cream cheese with a mixer and add one egg at a time beating well after each addition. Beat in cream, vanilla, and jam. Mix with the dry ingredients until moist but still lumpy. Mix the last four ingredients and sprinkle over top of the muffins. Bake for twenty to twenty-five minutes and cool a couple of minutes before removing from muffin tin.

Thyme and Lemon Tea Loaf

Makes one loaf

¾ cup milk
1 tbsp. minced fresh thyme
or 1 tsp. dried thyme
½ cup softened butter
1 cup sugar
2 eggs
2 cup flour
1½ tsp. baking powder
Pinch of salt
1 tbsp. lemon juice
1 tbsp. grated lemon peel

Preheat oven to 350 degrees. Combine milk and thyme in a bowl, and microwave, uncovered, for one to two minutes or until bubbly. Cover and cool to room temperature.

In large bowl, cream sugar and butter. Add eggs, one at a time, beating well after each one. Combine flour, baking powder, and salt; add to creamed mixture alternately with milk mixture. Stir in lemon juice and lemon peel.

Pour into 9" x 5" x 3" loaf pan. Bake for forty to forty-five minutes or until toothpick inserted near the center comes out clean. Cool for ten minutes before removing from pan.

In a small bowl, combine ½ cup icing sugar and 1 tbsp. Lemon juice and drizzle over loaf.

White Chocolate Pecan Muffins

Makes 6

1 ¾ cups flour
¾ cups sugar
2 ½ tsp. baking powder
½ tsp. salt
1 egg
1 cup milk
¼ cup butter, melted
¾ cup white chocolate chips
¾ cup chopped pecan nuts
Glaze
½ cup white chocolate chips
2 tbsp. whipping cream

Preheat oven to 400 degrees. In a bowl, combine flour, sugar, baking powder, and salt. In another bowl, whisk or beat the egg, milk, and butter. Stir into dry ingredients just until moistened. Fold in chocolate chips and nuts.

Fill muffin tins ¾ full and bake for fifteen to eighteen minutes. Cool for five minutes before removing to a wire rack to cool. Microwave chocolate chips and whipping cream, stirring until smooth and drizzle over the warm muffins.

Use a large muffin tin; large muffins look so much better than tiny ones. I prefer to spray my tins. I find digging at the paper cups a waste of time.

Exceptional Recipes -

Apple and Brie Omelet

Serves 1

1 ½ tbsp. butter
¼ medium size Granny Smith apple,
peeled and sliced thinly
⅛ tsp. ground nutmeg
1 tsp. sugar
1 tbsp. brown sugar
1 tbsp. chopped pecans
3 eggs
6 cubes (½") Brie cheese

In a heavy skillet, melt ½ tbsp. butter. Sauté apple slices in melted butter until glossy but not mushy. Sprinkle apples with nutmeg and sugar. Remove apples to a side dish and set aside. Mix together brown sugar and pecans; also set aside. In clean skillet, melt 1 tbsp. butter, heating until bubbly. Break eggs in a bowl and whisk until foamy; pour into skillet. As eggs begin to set, lift edges to let any uncooked liquid slide under. When eggs are almost set, turn off heat. Put Brie on one side of omelet and top with apples and fold in half. Allow to sit for two to three minutes to allow Brie to melt. Be sure to top with a brown sugar and pecan topping.

Apple Crepes with Calvados Butter Sauce

This is not as difficult as it may first appear, but it is another to-die-for recipe. Serves 6

Crepes:
4 beaten eggs
2 tbsp. sugar
½ cup melted butter
1 ½ cup flour
1 tsp. salt
¾ tsp. nutmeg
1 ⅔ cups milk

Butter Sauce:
6 tbsp. unsalted butter
½ cup sugar
¼ tsp. kosher salt
3 tbsp. Calvados

Apples:
2 tbsp. unsalted butter
2 medium Golden Delicious,
   peeled, cored, and
   cut in ⅓-inch cubes
3 tbsp. sugar
¼ tsp. kosher salt
¼ tsp. ground cinnamon
2–3 tbsp. Calvados

For Crepes:
Mix together first three ingredients: eggs, sugar, and butter. Mix in same bowl the dry ingredients, flour, salt, and nutmeg, alternating with milk. Combine all ingredients as above and pour into blender and blend until smooth. This can be made a day ahead and, if covered, refrigerated. Blend again before using.

Line plate with paper towel or parchment paper. Heat nine-inch nonstick skillet, with seven-inch diameter bottom, over medium heat. Add 2 tbsp. batter to skillet, tilt and rotate to spread batter evenly over the bottom. Cook until center of crepe is cooked through and edges are slightly browned (about a minute) Run spatula around crepe and invert onto plate. Repeat with remaining batter placing parchment paper between each crepe, making at least eighteen crepes.

For Butter Sauce:
Make in the morning. Put all ingredients in a pot and boil for ten to fifteen minutes and brush on crepes before folding.

For Apples:
Melt butter in a large skillet over medium heat. Add apples; sprinkle with sugar, salt and cinnamon. Sauté until tender (about three minutes).Add Calvados and cook most of the liquid away (about two minutes) Remove from heat and let stand at room temperature.

Preheat oven to 300 degrees. Place crepe stack on rimmed baking sheet (yes, keep the paper between the layers). Cover with a sheet of foil and seal the edges; warm in oven until heated through (about twenty minutes for cold crepes and fifteen minutes for room temperature).

Heat Calvados butter sauce in small saucepan until melted and heated through. Re-warm apple mixture over medium heat, stirring occasionally for about three minutes. Place one crepe on plate, browned side down. Spoon 2 tsp. Calvados sauce over crepe then fold crepe into quarters. Repeat with remaining crepes and butter sauce. Place three on a plate, spoon apples over crepe, and spoon any remaining sauce over crepes and serve.

Crustless Quiche

Serves 4

1 tbsp. unsalted butter
1 ½ cups shredded hash browns
½ cup frozen onions
1 cup diced cooked ham
8 oz. shredded Swiss cheese (2 cups)
4 large eggs
1 cup whipping cream
1 cup whole milk
½ tsp. pepper

Preheat oven to 425 degrees and place rack in the middle of the oven. Butter quiche dish and then sprinkle with hash browns. In a fry pan, cook onions with the ham stirring occasionally until pale golden or about five minutes. Spread in dish and sprinkle cheese on top. Whisk together eggs, cream, and milk with pepper and pour over cheese. Bake until golden and set in the center (twenty to twenty-five minutes). Cool slightly before cutting into wedges. Serve with fresh melon slices.

Bestest Waffles—Honest!

1 package of quick-rising yeast
1 tbsp. sugar
2 cups warm milk (approx. 110 degrees)
4 eggs, separated
1 tsp. pure vanilla extract
2 ½ cups flour
¼ tsp. salt
¼ tsp. ground nutmeg
½ cup melted butter

In a mixing bowl, dissolve yeast and sugar in warmed milk. Beat yolks lightly and add to the yeast mixture along with the vanilla. Combine flour, salt, and nutmeg; stir into yeast mixture until moistened, Add butter and mix well. Beat egg whites until stiff peaks form, then fold into the batter. Cover and let rise until doubled (about forty-five minutes). Bake in a preheated waffle iron until golden. Top with warm pure maple syrup or your own homemade fruit syrup. I say top, but we use individual boats for the syrup to allow guests to use as much or as little as they like. Also, each guest has his or her own butter dish.

Creamed Eggs with Smoked Salmon in Puff Pastry

Makes 4

4 puff pastry shells
8 large eggs
2 tbsp. butter
4–6 tbsp. chopped salmon (or ham if you wish)
2 tbsp. each of chopped red and green bell peppers
2 tbsp. sour cream
Hollandaise sauce mix (we can cheat here)
Parsley or paprika (optional)

Bake puff pastry shells as directed on package. Cool and prepare for serving.

Beat eggs until light and fluffy. In fry pan, melt butter, and then add salmon and peppers. Sauté until barely limp. Add eggs, cooking and stirring until almost done. Add sour cream and stir. Do not let eggs get too dry, but remove from heat while still creamy. Spoon mixture into each pastry shell, allowing some of the egg mixture to flow onto the plate. Cover with two to three tbsp of sauce, and then sprinkle with parsley or paprika. Serve with fresh fruit in season (melon is excellent).

Eggs Benedict (Don's Way)

Serves two hungry people or four light eaters.

2 English muffins
4 thick slices of Canadian bacon or smoked salmon lox, warmed
4 eggs
Hollandaise Sauce (recipe follows)

Split, toast, and lightly butter English muffins. Place the s slices of cooked bacon or smoked salmon lox on top of each English muffin. Poach eggs in boiling water (make sure you pour a little vinegar in the water so they don't float all over the pan). When eggs are cooked (not over cooked), place on top of English muffins. Top with Hollandaise sauce.

Sauce
3 egg yolks
Pinch of salt
Pinch of white sugar
3 drops of Tabasco sauce
⅛ tsp. dry mustard
Juice of half a lemon
¾ cup butter

Combine first six ingredients in a blender; blend on high to mix. Microwave butter until melted. Turn blender on high and slowly pour the butter into the yolk mixture in a steady stream until all is added. When reheating, use hot, never boiling, water.
Garnish the plate with a bit of parsley, a slice of melon, or star fruit.

French Toast–Baked

4 slices thick toast
6 large eggs
1 cups milk
1 ½ cups whipping cream
1 tsp. vanilla
¼ tsp. cinnamon

¼ tsp. ground nutmeg
(fresh ground is best)
¼ cup butter
½ cup packed brown sugar
1 tbsp. light corn syrup

Serves 2

Butter a 9" square baking pan. Overlap slices to completely fill pan. In a medium bowl, combine eggs, milk, whipping cream, vanilla, cinnamon, and nutmeg, mixing well. Pour over bread then cover and put in fridge overnight.

In the morning, remove from fridge forty-five minutes before baking and preheat oven to 350 degrees. In a small bowl, combine last three items and after mixing well, spread over bread. Bake forty-five to sixty minutes until puffed and golden. Serve with warm syrup of your choice.

French Toast with Pears and Pomegranate Sauce

Serves 2

3 large eggs
½ cup whole milk
2 tsp. pure vanilla extract
¾ tsp. cardamom, divided
2 slices thick bread

4 tbsp. butter, divided
½ cup pomegranate juice
⅓ cup packed brown sugar
1 ripe, but still firm, red Anjou pear,
cut into thin slices

Whisk together eggs, milk, vanilla, and ½ cardamom and pour into 9-inch square glass baking dish. Add bread and let stand about ten minutes, turning over with a spatula until mixture is absorbed. Melt 1 tbsp. butter in a fry pan over medium heat. Add pear. Sauté for about three minutes until soft. Transfer to plate. Add 2 tbsp. butter to fry pan; add juice, brown sugar, and cardamom simmering until thickens and syrupy (five minutes). Remove from heat. Melt remaining butter on griddle, add bread slices and cook until golden (about three minutes each side), cut in half, and divide onto plates. Top with pears, spoon sauce on top. Serve.

Gingerbread Pancakes

Serves 2–4

Lemon Sauce
1 cup sugar
2 tbsp. cornstarch
½ cup water
¼ cup butter
2 tbsp. grated lemon rind
¼ cup lemon juice

Pancakes
1 cup milk
5 large eggs
2 tsp. molasses
1 ½ cups flour
¼ tsp. salt
2 tbsp. sugar
2 tsp. ground ginger
1 tsp. cinnamon
½ tsp. nutmeg
¼ tsp. ground cloves
6 tbsp. butter
Enough water to make pancake
batter (2 cups plus)

Sauce
Combine sugar and cornstarch in saucepan. Gradually stir in water, bringing to a boil. Cook, stirring constantly for five minutes, or until thickened. Remove from heat; add butter, lemon rind, and lemon juice. Mix well. Keep warm.

Pancakes
In a large bowl, beat milk and eggs together. Add molasses and 2 tbsp. water and stir. Mix the dry ingredients, cut in butter until mixture is coarse crumbs, then add to wet mix, adding additional water until batter is smooth. Heat griddle and oil it if necessary. Pour batter onto hot griddle. When bubbles form on surface, flip and brown the other side.

Gingerbread Waffles

Waffles
1 cup flour
1 ½ tsp. baking powder
1 tsp. ground ginger
¾ tsp. ground cinnamon
½ tsp. ground allspice
½ tsp. baking soda
¼ tsp. dry mustard
¼ tsp. salt
⅓ cup packed brown sugar
1 egg, separated
¼ molasses
¾ cup buttermilk
3 tbsp. melted butter
⅓ cup chopped pecans
⅛ tsp. cream of tartar

Topping
1 tbsp. candied ginger
1 ½ cups whipping cream

In a bowl combine the first eight ingredients. In a large mixing bowl, beat the brown sugar with the egg yolk until fluffy. Now add molasses, buttermilk, and butter. Stir into dry ingredients until combined. Add the pecans.
In a small bowl, beat egg whites and cream of tartar until soft peaks form. Gently fold into batter.
Bake in a preheated waffle iron until golden brown. In a blender, chop candied ginger until fine. Whip cream until stiff peaks form and fold in the candied ginger. Top waffles while still warm.

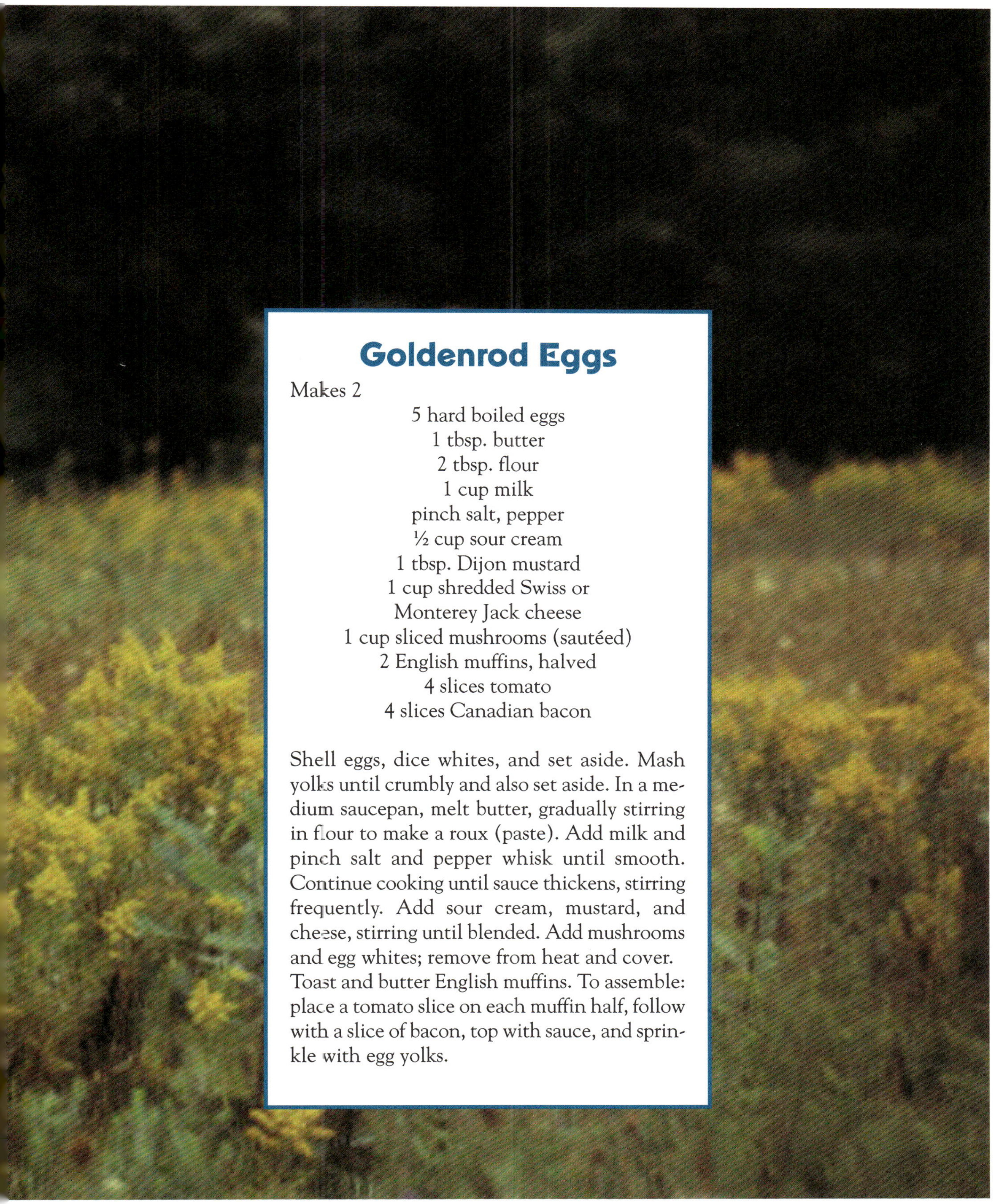

Goldenrod Eggs

Makes 2

5 hard boiled eggs
1 tbsp. butter
2 tbsp. flour
1 cup milk
pinch salt, pepper
½ cup sour cream
1 tbsp. Dijon mustard
1 cup shredded Swiss or
Monterey Jack cheese
1 cup sliced mushrooms (sautéed)
2 English muffins, halved
4 slices tomato
4 slices Canadian bacon

Shell eggs, dice whites, and set aside. Mash yolks until crumbly and also set aside. In a medium saucepan, melt butter, gradually stirring in flour to make a roux (paste). Add milk and pinch salt and pepper whisk until smooth. Continue cooking until sauce thickens, stirring frequently. Add sour cream, mustard, and cheese, stirring until blended. Add mushrooms and egg whites; remove from heat and cover. Toast and butter English muffins. To assemble: place a tomato slice on each muffin half, follow with a slice of bacon, top with sauce, and sprinkle with egg yolks.

Ham and Swiss Stuffed Puff Pastry

Serves 2

1 sheet frozen puff pastry
1 tbsp. Dijon mustard
Slices of cooked ham
Slices Swiss cheese
1 beaten egg
1 tbsp. cream

Preheat oven to 400 degrees. Unfold pastry. When thawed, divide into four squares. Spread mustard over each square, place ham and cheese on top, and fold into a triangle. Wet the edges with cream and seal closed. Put on cookie sheet and bake for about fifteen to twenty minutes until puffed and golden brown. Serve hot with scrambled eggs and freshly baked muffins.

**Lemon-Scented Blueberry Pancakes
with Warm Blueberry Sauce**

Lemon-Scented Blueberry Pancakes
with Warm Blueberry Sauce

Serves 2

Sauce
1 pint fresh blueberries (stemmed, hulled)
2 cups light corn syrup

Pancakes
1 cup flour
2 tbsp. sugar
1 tsp. baking powder
½ tsp. baking soda
Pinch of salt
1 cup buttermilk
1 large egg
2 tbsp. melted butter
2 tbsp. fresh grated lemon zest
Icing sugar (optional)

In a non-reactive saucepan over medium heat, combine berries and syrup. Bring to a boil and cook for two minutes. Remove from heat and with a fork, mash the fruit. Keep warm.
In a small bowl, sift flour, sugar, baking powder, baking soda, and salt. In another bowl whisk buttermilk, egg, and butter until well blended. Add the dry ingredients to the buttermilk mixture and whisk until slightly smooth, but still having some lumps. Fold in lemon zest and allow batter to sit for a few minutes. Lightly grease griddle over medium heat. In small batches pour ¼ cup batter onto hot griddle and cook for two to three minutes until batter bubbles and is golden brown. Repeat for the remaining batter. Put three to four pancakes on each plate and drizzle with warm blueberry sauce.

Orange Croissant French Toast

This is very showy and very elegant and exceptionally fine cuisine. This has real WOW factor
Serves 3–4

6 large eggs
1 ½ cups heavy cream or half and half
2–3 tsp. Grand Marnier
1 tsp. pure vanilla extract
½ tsp. ground cinnamon
Pinch of ground nutmeg
Pinch of salt
Grated zest of one orange
4 oz. cream cheese
2 tbsp. icing sugar
4 croissants (one day old)
½ cup orange marmalade
2 tbsp. unsalted butter
2 tbsp. Crisco oil
Orange syrup (recipe follows)
2 segmented oranges

Preheat oven to 250 degrees. Whisk eggs, cream, Grand Marnier, vanilla, cinnamon, nutmeg, salt, and orange zest in a medium bowl. Now stir together cream cheese and icing sugar in a separate small bowl.

Cut croissant in half, lengthwise. Spread outside bottom with cream cheese mixture, then spread outside top half with marmalade. Place back together (they will be inverted with cut side out) to seal. Place the stuffed croissants in a shallow baking dish large enough to hold them in a single layer. Pour egg mixture over croissant and soak for five minutes. Turn over and soak for another five minutes or until they are soaked through.

Heat 1 tbsp. butter and 1 tbsp. Crisco oil in a large skillet over medium heat. Fry half of the croissant for about three minutes until golden brown.

Place a wire rack on a baking sheet. Transfer fried croissants to wire rack and place in oven while cooking the remaining croissants. Wipe out skillet and repeat with remaining oil, butter, and croissants.

Serve warm with orange syrup and orange segments.

Orange Syrup
1 cup sugar
½ cup water
¾ cup orange juice
1 tbsp. cornstarch
2 tbsp. unsalted butter

Combine the sugar and water in a small saucepan and bring to a boil, stirring until sugar dissolves. Combine juice and cornstarch in a bowl and then mix into sugar syrup. Simmer gently until thick. (About six to eight minutes) Add butter and stir until it melts. Serve warm over croissants.

Puffiest Cheese Omelet Ever

This is so impressive you will want to make it for yourself on Sunday morning and read the paper in your jammies, watch old movies—whatever reason you want to dream up.

Serves 2

2 large eggs, separated
Pinch of fresh ground nutmeg
Salt and pepper to taste
½ cup sour cream
1 tbsp. butter
¾ cup pepper jack cheese
(or Balderson's aged cheddar)

Preheat oven to 350 degrees. In medium bowl, beat egg whites until stiff, moist peaks form. (My husband does this with a whisk and a copper bowl. I mention this because his arms ache afterwards. It is quite a workout.) In another bowl, beat yolks with a touch of salt, pepper, and nutmeg until thick and lemon coloured. Whisk in sour cream. Pour yolk mixture over beaten egg whites and GENTLY fold together. Melt butter in a ten-inch, oven-proof frying pan over medium heat. Tilt to cover the bottom of the pan and then pour in egg mixture.

Do not stir, but cook until omelet is puffy and lightly browned on the bottom. This takes two to three minutes. Transfer pan to oven and bake until top is a pale golden brown (takes six to nine minutes) and a knife, when inserted, comes out clean. Sprinkle with cheese. Using a spatula, fold half the omelet over the other half. Slide omelet onto a warm plate and serve immediately. This can be cut in two as it is quite a generous serving.

To take it up a notch, add pre-steamed asparagus, red peppers, or mushrooms before folding over the top edge.

Puffy Cheese Strata

Serves 4

Using a 13" x 9" pan, use enough crustless bread
slices to make a double layer.
½ lb. Balderson's white cheddar cheese
¾ lb. grated Monterey Jack cheese
(extra for later)
8 large eggs
2 cups milk
½ cup whipping cream
Fresh parsley

Place one layer of bread in the baking pan. Grate both cheeses, and then sprinkle ⅓ of cheese mixture on top of bread slices. Add a second layer of bread. Now blend the eggs, milk, and whipping cream, then pour over the bread slices. Top with remaining cheese mixture. Cover and refrigerate overnight, allowing the milk to puff up the bread. Take the baking pan out of the fridge. Preheat oven to 350 degrees. Bake covered for about twenty minutes. Take cover off and continue baking another twenty minutes. When done, it should be really puffy and just starting to turn a golden brown. Cut into eight pieces and garnish with fresh parsley.

Pumpkin Waffles with Apple Cider Syrup

2 ½ cups flour
4 tsp. baking powder
2 tsp. ground cinnamon
1 tsp. ground allspice
1 tsp. ground ginger
½ tsp. salt
¼ cup brown sugar
1 cup canned pure pumpkin
2 cups milk
4 eggs, separated
¼ cup melted butter

Syrup
½ cup white sugar
1 tbsp. cornstarch
1 tsp. ground cinnamon
1 cup apple cider
1 tbsp. lemon juice
2 tbsp. butter

Preheat waffle iron. Combine first seven ingredients in a bowl. In a separate bowl, stir together pumpkin, milk, and egg yolks. Whip egg whites until soft peaks form.

Stir the dry ingredients plus melted butter into the pumpkin mixture, stirring just to combine. Fold in ⅓ of the egg whites, stirring until incorporated. Fold in remaining whites. Cook waffles until golden brown. Stir together the sugar, cornstarch, and cinnamon in a saucepan. Stir in the cider and lemon juice. Cook over medium heat just until the mixture begins to boil. Continue until the syrup thickens, then stir in 2 tbsp. butter until melted. Serve warm with the waffles.

Quiche Holly Arch

Serve with warm muffins and freshly brewed coffee Serves 4

1–9" unbaked pie shell from frozen puff pastry
2 tsp. butter
12 slices bacon, chopped
1 large red pepper, seeded, diced small
2 cups whipping cream
(of course, it's good for you)
4 large eggs
½ tsp. salt
Pinch of cayenne pepper
½ tsp onion powder (not real onion)
1 cup grated Swiss cheese

Preheat oven to 425 degrees. Sauté bacon until crisp. Beat cream, eggs, and spices until well mixed. Sprinkle pie shell with bacon, red pepper, and cheese. Pour egg mixture carefully on top. Bake at 425 degrees for fifteen minutes, then reduce heat to 300 degrees and bake for approximately forty minutes or until knife inserted in the centre comes out clean.

We opted for the red pepper rather than onions (which I don't eat; several of our guests request no onions in anything.) The flavour is really nice, and yes, the man in your life will enjoy it.

Swiss Eggs

My husband and I had discussions about putting this recipe up for our guests. It was the first breakfast my husband made for me, telling me it was one of his mother's favourite dishes. I have not let him use this recipe for anyone except me for almost twenty years and he now says, and I quote,

"If the B & B is our B & B, then I must use this recipe." Lucky you! Here it is.

Makes 2

Cheese Sauce
5–6 tbsp. Cheese Whiz
5–6 tbsp. cream cheese
½ cup milk (cream is better, but richer)
2 English muffins
4 large eggs

Melt Cheese Whiz over medium heat in a fry pan; slowly add the cream cheese, stirring constantly to a smooth consistency. Add milk and combine.

Crack four eggs and gently immerse in the cheese sauce. The method here is to poach the eggs, not fry them. When the tops are cooked, but still soft, place on toasted English muffins. Spoon the sauce over eggs. (As you can see, this one is hard for me to let go.)

Index

Watch for An Exceptional Cookbook with an Extraordinary Lead In to Christmas

coming out soon